Exploring
CAMBODIA

Dr. Diana Prince

AuthorHouse™
1663 Liberty Drive
Bloomington, IN 47403
www.authorhouse.com
Phone: 833-262-8899

This book is printed on acid-free paper.

ISBN: 979-8-8230-2891-2 (sc)
ISBN: 979-8-8230-2893-6 (hc)
ISBN: 979-8-8230-2892-9 (e)

Library of Congress Control Number: 2024912577

Print information available on the last page.

Published by AuthorHouse 08/07/2024

authorHOUSE

Exploring
CAMBODIA

Introduction

This book explores the country of Cambodia, with its roots in the ancient past. It is a photographic journey of this remarkable country. The first section focuses on the *Temples of Angkor Wat*. The second section focuses on the *People and Places of Cambodia*.

Cambodia has experienced a difficult and turbulent past. It is important to acknowledge the very real challenges that have shaped the country today. This book explores Cambodia today, and the new generation of men and women who are shaping that future.

Cambodia is located in Southeast Asia, encompassing the Mekong Delta and a sprawling landscape that also includes vast plains, forests and mountains. The Khmer Empire dates to 800 AD, and its first king Jayavarman who united the warring tribes in the region. Cambodia's current population is 17 million people. Today, the country has a parliament and constitution, as well as a monarch, who is elected. King Sihamoni is the current king.

In the Tenth Century, the Angkor Empire had reached its zenith. It was a rich country known for its lavish shrines, thriving trade and agricultural resources. In the late 1800's, it was a protectorate under the French. During World War II, it was occupied by the Japanese. In this century, Cambodia achieved independence from France in 1953.

Soon after this, the Communist Khmer Rouge regime seized the country. They executed nearly 2 million Cambodians. This terror was carried out under the regime leader named Pol Pot. A very dark episode in the history of Cambodia is linked to the "Killing Fields". This refers to the national genocide in which over one million people were killed during the era of the rule by the Khmer Rouge. The conflict began in 1975 and lasted for four years. While most of the deaths were the result of Communist execution, another two million deaths were caused by starvation and rampant disease. The killing did not stop until Vietnam invaded the country in 1978, defeating the ruling regime of the Khmer Rouge under the dictator Pol Pot.

The next 20 years witnessed both the occupation by the Vietnamese, and an internal civil war. The Paris Peace Accord in 1991, and the United Nations intervention two years later, restored a constitutional government.

Today, Cambodia is well known for the city of Angkor Wat, built in the Twelfth Century during the Khmer Empire. Its name means "City of Temples". This complex of over 300 temples is the largest religious complex in the world. UNESCO reports that about 5,000 elephants were involved in the construction of this elaborate complex at Angkor Wat. Today it is estimated that less than 400 elephants occupy Cambodia's forests.

The Ancient Temples of Angkor Wat

North Entry Gate at Angkor Wat

Three Temple Shrines

Spring Morning in Cambodia (A)

Spring Morning in Cambodia (B)

Ancient Stone Road Inside Angkor Wat

Hillside Shrines

Lion Sentinels in Stone

Bayon Temple

Earthquake Damage

Stone Altar Inside Shrine

Elephants for Transportation

Morning Sentinels

Elephant Drivers Wait for Customers

Silent Sentinel at Entryway

Early Morning in Angkor Wat

Shadows in Time

Ta Prohm Temple Engulfed by Ancient Trees

Temple Competing with the Ravages of Time

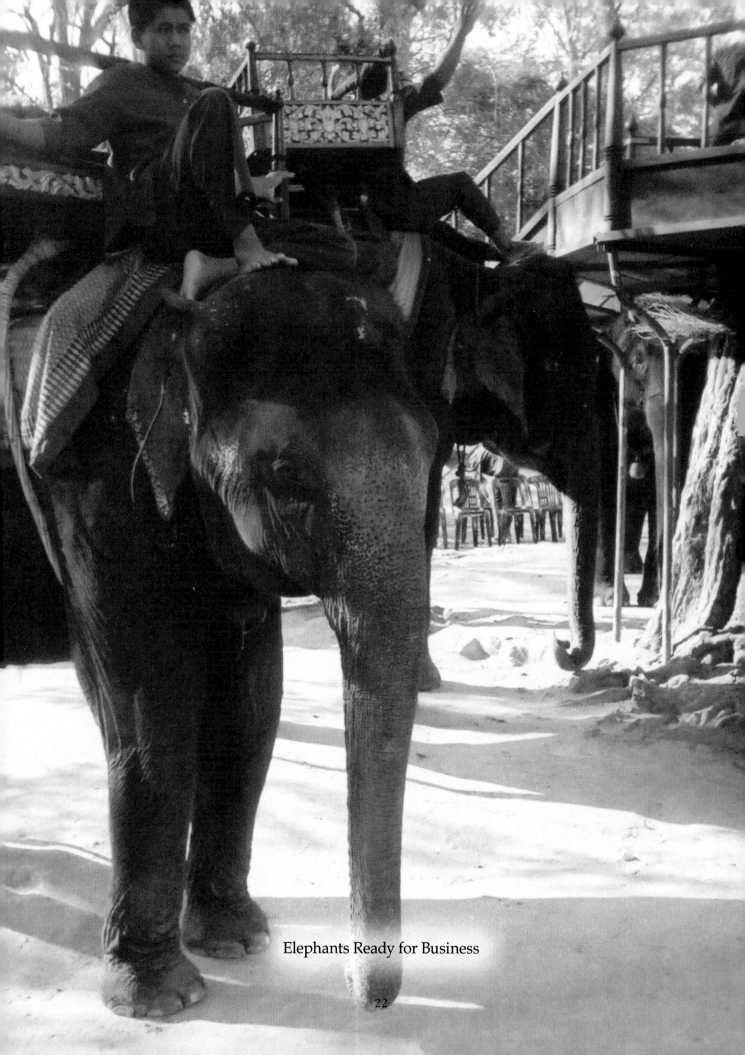

Elephants Ready for Business

Ta Prohm Temple and Ancient Roots

Visitors at Ta Prohm Temple

Sun and Shadows

Ancient Faces of Time

Ritual on Temple Grounds

Visitors Dwarfed by Massive Temple

Ancient God in Sunlit Temple

Angkor Wat Reflecting Lake in the Morning

Visitors Navigate Steep Stairway

Stone Pathway

Three Women on Temple Step

Ancient Tree at Ta Prohm Temple

Faces in Stone

Ta Prohm Temple at Sunset

Stone Lions Guard Temple Grounds

Author at Ta Prohm Temple

Ancient Roots

Ancient Altar

Tourists at Ta Prohm Temple

Roots Cling to Ancient Wall

Tourists Navigate Temple Steps

Remains of Sacrificial Site

Sunset Falls on Ancient Ruins

45

Reflecting Lake at Angkor Wat

Navigating Ancient Ruins

Visitors Dwarfed by Gigantic Tree Roots

The Longest Climb

Early Morning Visitors at Angkor Wat

Ancient Stones of Bayon Temple

Bayon Temple

Ceremony Inside Temple

53

Early Morning at Angkor Wat

Temple Showing Ravages of Time

Young Girl and her Brother at Angkor Wat

Sunset at Angkor Wat

People and Places in Cambodia

In this village called Kampong Phluk, the houses are built on stilts. Located near Siem Reap, this village is located next to Lake Tonle Sap, Cambodia's largest lake. The people who live here are employed in the fishing industry, or working in the nearby rice fields.

Young Woman near Lake Tonle Sap

Pigs in a pen at Kampong Phluk

Apple Cart in Village outside Phnom Penh

House on Stilts near Tonle Sap Lake

Young Village Girl in Kampong Phluk

Young Boy in Fishing Village of Kampong Phluk

Family in House Built on Stilts next to Lake Tonle Sap

66

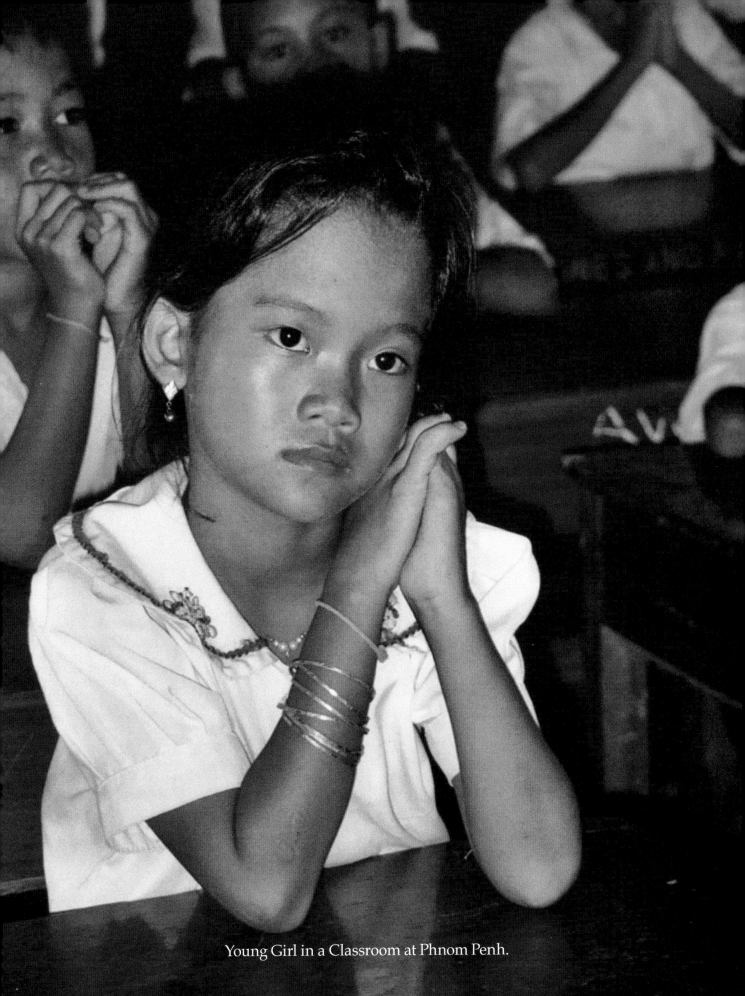

Young Girl in a Classroom at Phnom Penh.

Young Girl and her Brother near Tonle Sap Lake

Morning Begins on Tonle Sap Lake.

Young Girls Greet Visitors at Tonle Sap Lake

Young Village Girls Pose at their village near Tonle Sap Lake

Girl with her Young Brother

Late Afternoon on Tonle Sap Lake

Crocodiles Lurking Under a House Built on Stilts

Early Morning on the Tonle Sap Lake

Two Young Boys Afloat in the Tonle Sap Lake

Shy Girl in Front of Her Home

Oxen Resting

Oxen Beginning their Work Day

Young Brothers Waving from their River Home

Young Girl Near Tonle Sap Lake

Classroom near Tonle Sap Lake

Classroom near Tonle Sap Lake

Young Girl Grocery Shopping with her Mother

84

Young Girl at Home on Tonle Sap Lake

Teenagers at Tonle Sap

Meal Preparation

Morning Chores Begin Near the Lake

Young Boy in a Local Shop

Children Playing

Students at a religious school say morning prayers in Phnom Penh.

Mother and Child in their Home by the River

House Built on Stilts Overlooks a Vast Lily Pond

Hearth inside a Village Home

Young Mother with her Two Children

Brilliant Pink Water Lilies in Bloom

Oxen Being Prepared for the Day's Work

Author with Village Children

Palace Grounds at Phnom Penh

A Sea of Water Lilies

The skulls in this enclosure are from prisoners executed at the "Killing Fields". This monument is located at the "Choeung Ek Site" near Phnom Penh. Remains of over 8,000 victims were unearthed in this location.

Near the remains of the victims killed in the massacre by
the Khmer Rouge from 1975 through 1979, there are photos
which were identified as some of those victims.

Wat Thmey Temple at Siem Reap was an execution site from 1975 to 1979. Over two million people perished in these killings under the Khmer Rouge regime of Pol Pot.

The Silver Pagoda at the Royal Palace Complex near Phnom Penh

The End

Printed in the United States
by Baker & Taylor Publisher Services